Insects

CONTENTS

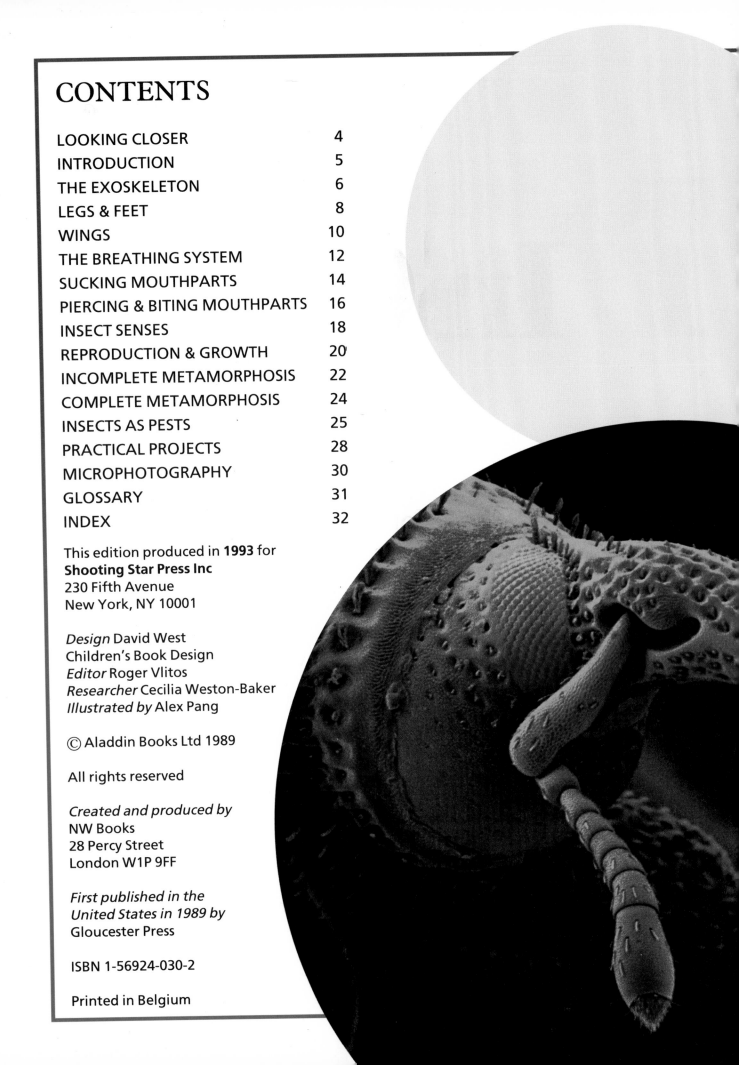

LOOKING CLOSER   4
INTRODUCTION   5
THE EXOSKELETON   6
LEGS & FEET   8
WINGS   10
THE BREATHING SYSTEM   12
SUCKING MOUTHPARTS   14
PIERCING & BITING MOUTHPARTS   16
INSECT SENSES   18
REPRODUCTION & GROWTH   20
INCOMPLETE METAMORPHOSIS 22
COMPLETE METAMORPHOSIS   24
INSECTS AS PESTS   25
PRACTICAL PROJECTS   28
MICROPHOTOGRAPHY   30
GLOSSARY   31
INDEX   32

This edition produced in **1993** for
Shooting Star Press Inc
230 Fifth Avenue
New York, NY 10001

Design David West
Children's Book Design
Editor Roger Vlitos
Researcher Cecilia Weston-Baker
Illustrated by Alex Pang

© Aladdin Books Ltd 1989

Created and produced by
NW Books
28 Percy Street
London W1P 9FF

*First published in the
United States in 1989 by*
Gloucester Press

ISBN 1-56924-030-2

Printed in Belgium

THROUGH · THE · MICROSCOPE

Insects

John Stidworthy

SHOOTING STAR PRESS

LOOKING CLOSER

Microscopes and magnifying glasses work by using lenses and light. A lens is usually a thin, circular glass, thicker in the middle, which bends rays of light so that when you look through it an object appears enlarged. A microscope uses several lenses. It will also have a set of adjustments to give you a choice of how much you want to magnify.

When we want to view something under a microscope it must be small enough to fit on a glass slide. This is put on the stage over the mirror and light is reflected through so that the lenses inside can magnify the view for us. But not all microscopes work this way. The greatest detail can be seen with an electron microscope which uses electron beams and electromagnets.

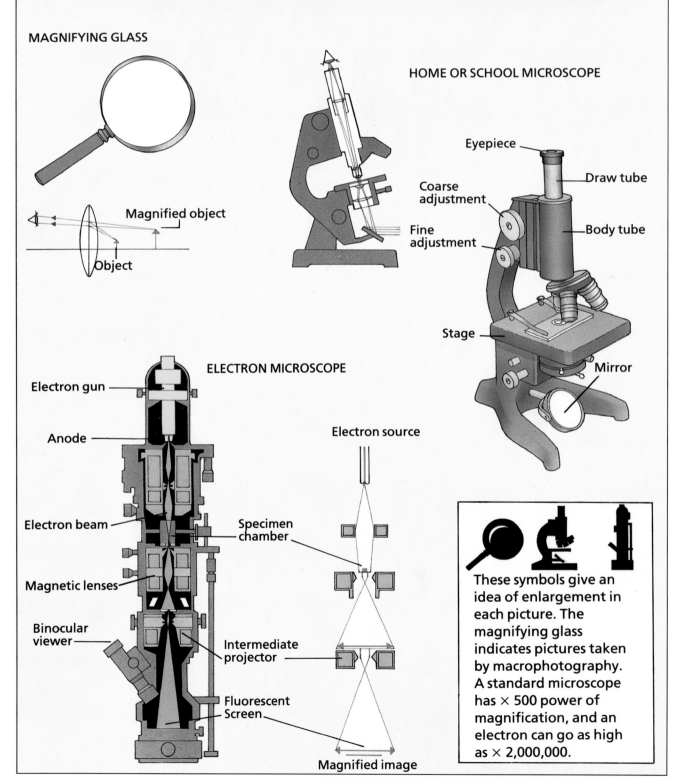

MAGNIFYING GLASS

Magnified object

Object

HOME OR SCHOOL MICROSCOPE

Eyepiece

Draw tube

Coarse adjustment

Fine adjustment

Body tube

Stage

Mirror

ELECTRON MICROSCOPE

Electron gun

Anode

Electron beam

Magnetic lenses

Binocular viewer

Electron source

Specimen chamber

Intermediate projector

Fluorescent Screen

Magnified image

These symbols give an idea of enlargement in each picture. The magnifying glass indicates pictures taken by macrophotography. A standard microscope has × 500 power of magnification, and an electron can go as high as × 2,000,000.

INTRODUCTION

This book contains photos of insects taken through microscopes or with close-up lenses on cameras. Next to each picture is a symbol showing how each was made. This will give you an idea of the amount of times each has been enlarged or magnified more than life-size.

Illustrations are included to help you understand what is being shown. We look in turn at the various body systems and aspects of insects, as shown below. You can see the complexity and beauty of the structures that make up the bodies of these small and fascinating creatures.

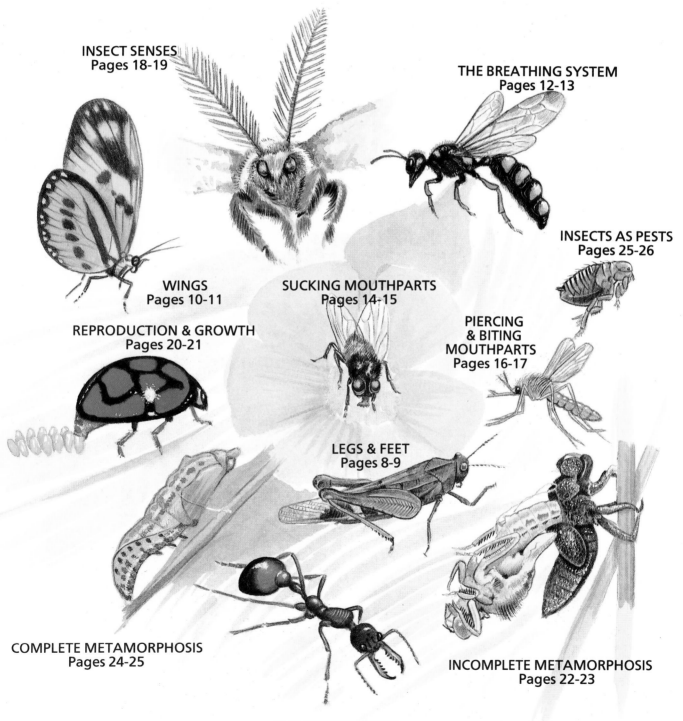

INSECT SENSES
Pages 18-19

THE BREATHING SYSTEM
Pages 12-13

INSECTS AS PESTS
Pages 25-26

WINGS
Pages 10-11

SUCKING MOUTHPARTS
Pages 14-15

PIERCING & BITING MOUTHPARTS
Pages 16-17

REPRODUCTION & GROWTH
Pages 20-21

LEGS & FEET
Pages 8-9

COMPLETE METAMORPHOSIS
Pages 24-25

INCOMPLETE METAMORPHOSIS
Pages 22-23

THE EXOSKELETON
Pages 6-7

EXOSKELETON

There are no bones in the body of an insect. Instead it has an exoskeleton, or "outside skeleton," which shapes, supports and protects it. This skin is made of a tough, light material called chitin, a substance related to sugar. Sometimes this is very thin, but it can be thickened to form a kind of armor if needed. A covering of waxy layers makes the exoskeleton watertight, so that it seldom lets moisture leak either in or out. Some insects have smooth exoskeletons. Others are covered with bumps, grooves, or even ornaments. If we take a closer look at the body of an insect with a magnifying glass we will see a large number of tiny hairs which are called setae. Some of them actually work as sense organs.

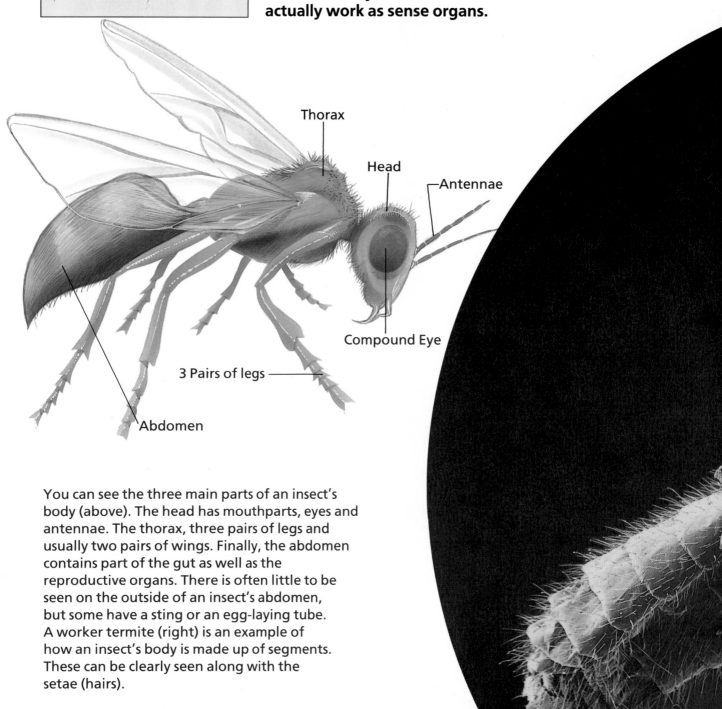

Thorax

Head

Antennae

Compound Eye

3 Pairs of legs

Abdomen

You can see the three main parts of an insect's body (above). The head has mouthparts, eyes and antennae. The thorax, three pairs of legs and usually two pairs of wings. Finally, the abdomen contains part of the gut as well as the reproductive organs. There is often little to be seen on the outside of an insect's abdomen, but some have a sting or an egg-laying tube. A worker termite (right) is an example of how an insect's body is made up of segments. These can be clearly seen along with the setae (hairs).

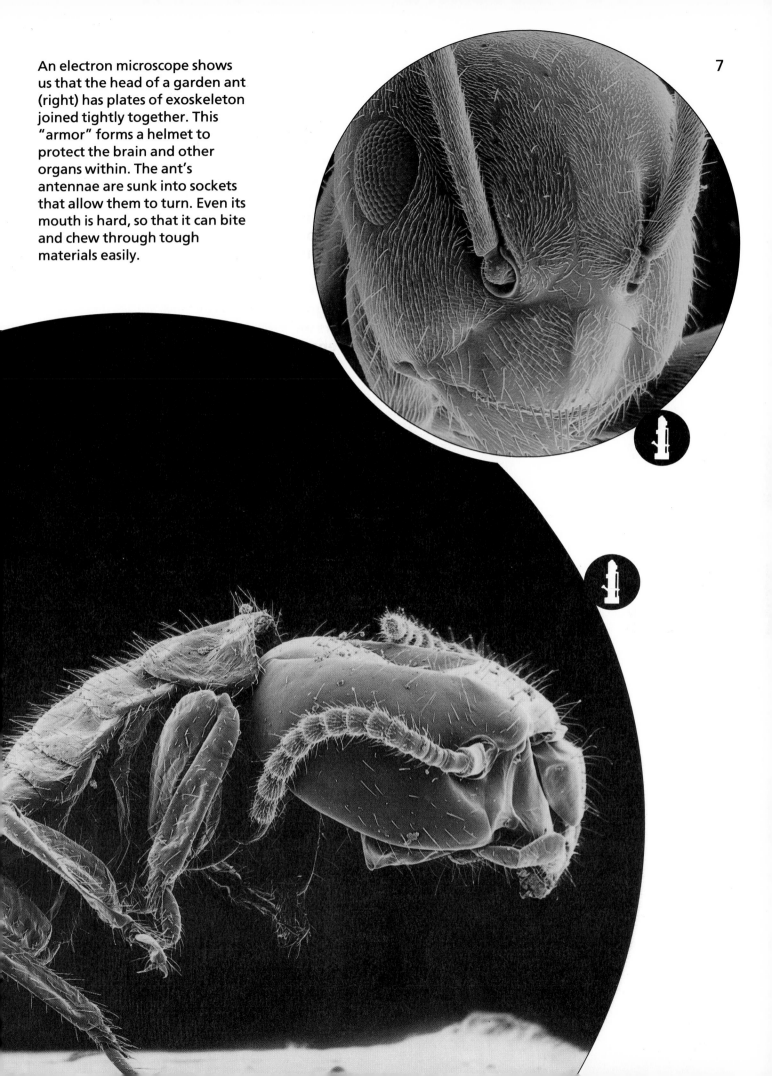

An electron microscope shows us that the head of a garden ant (right) has plates of exoskeleton joined tightly together. This "armor" forms a helmet to protect the brain and other organs within. The ant's antennae are sunk into sockets that allow them to turn. Even its mouth is hard, so that it can bite and chew through tough materials easily.

LEGS AND FEET

The legs of all adult insects are made the same way, with five main sections. There are two small sections close to the body, then a "femur" and "tibia" which are often long. At the end is the foot, or "tarsus." But if you look closely at several types of insects you will see that their legs are shaped for different jobs. A locust or grasshopper, for example, is a jumper. The back legs are very long, and can be straightened suddenly. This enables the creature to leap. Some swimming beetles have wide legs with long setae that work as paddles in the water. Bees have special patches of setae on their legs to gather and hold pollen. These details on insect legs can be seen best with either a magnifying glass or a standard microscope.

The feet of most insects end in a pair of claws which often have a pad between them. On the fly's foot illustrated below we can see two sticky pads (called pulvilli) which help it to climb glass or walk upside down on a ceiling. The caterpillar (above-right) has five pairs of "pro-legs," on its abdomen, each with a hook at the end, as well as the three true legs on its thorax.

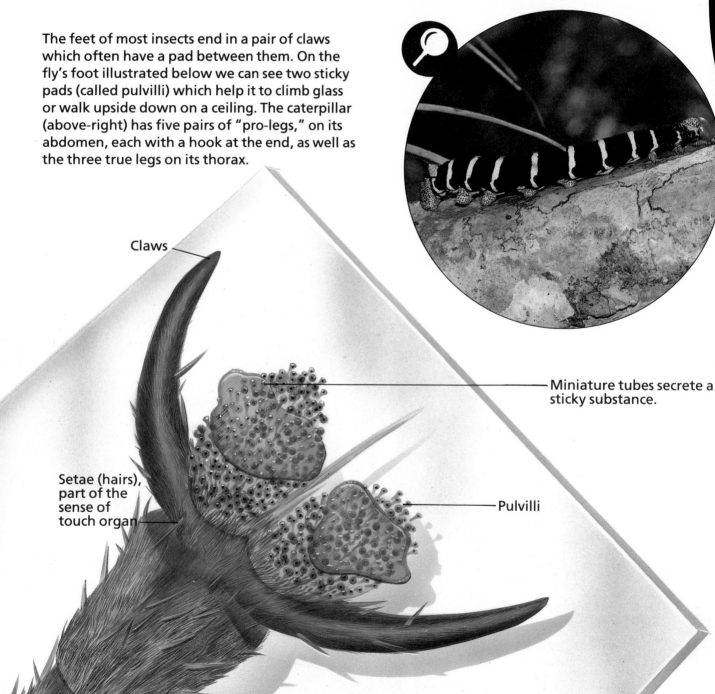

Claws

Miniature tubes secrete a sticky substance.

Setae (hairs), part of the sense of touch organ

Pulvilli

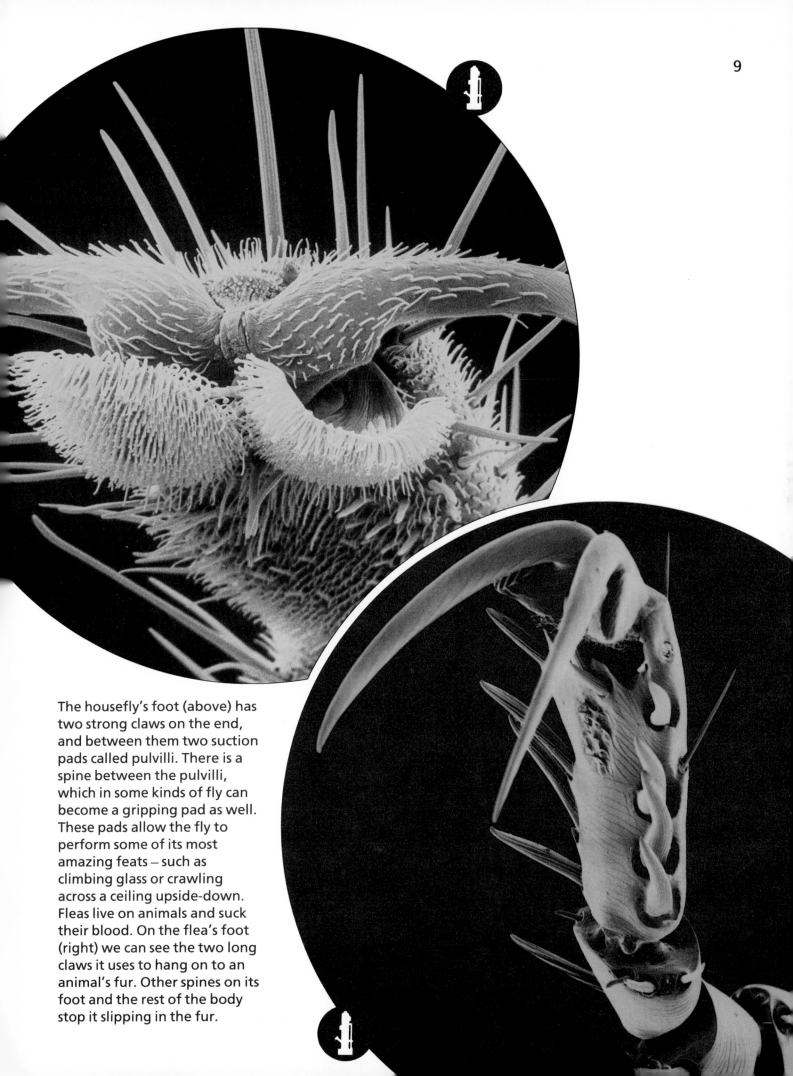

The housefly's foot (above) has two strong claws on the end, and between them two suction pads called pulvilli. There is a spine between the pulvilli, which in some kinds of fly can become a gripping pad as well. These pads allow the fly to perform some of its most amazing feats – such as climbing glass or crawling across a ceiling upside-down. Fleas live on animals and suck their blood. On the flea's foot (right) we can see the two long claws it uses to hang on to an animal's fur. Other spines on its foot and the rest of the body stop it slipping in the fur.

WINGS

The wings of all adult insects have the same basic structure. They are made of thin skin stretched over hollow but strong tubes called veins. Most insects have two pairs of wings which flap together at the same time. Some even have hooks to connect them, as can be seen on certain moths. However, a dragonfly uses each pair of wings separately so that it can hover. Beetles and cockroaches, on the other hand, have front wings which are more like stiff leather covers for their rear ones. They do not flap, but stick out in flight and steady their heavy bodies (see below). Houseflies are different again, and use only their front wings to fly. The rear ones look like pins but are sense organs used to keep them flying level.

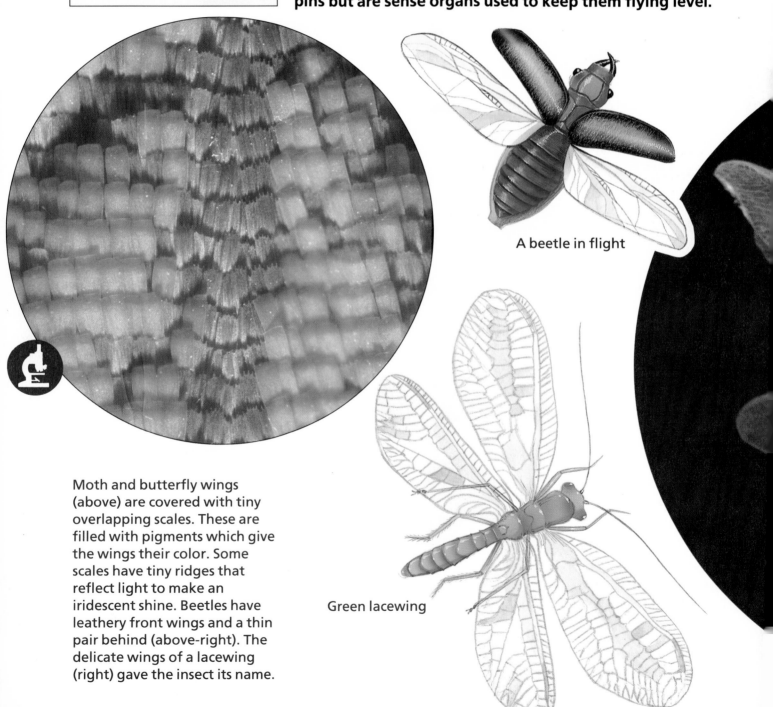

A beetle in flight

Green lacewing

Moth and butterfly wings (above) are covered with tiny overlapping scales. These are filled with pigments which give the wings their color. Some scales have tiny ridges that reflect light to make an iridescent shine. Beetles have leathery front wings and a thin pair behind (above-right). The delicate wings of a lacewing (right) gave the insect its name.

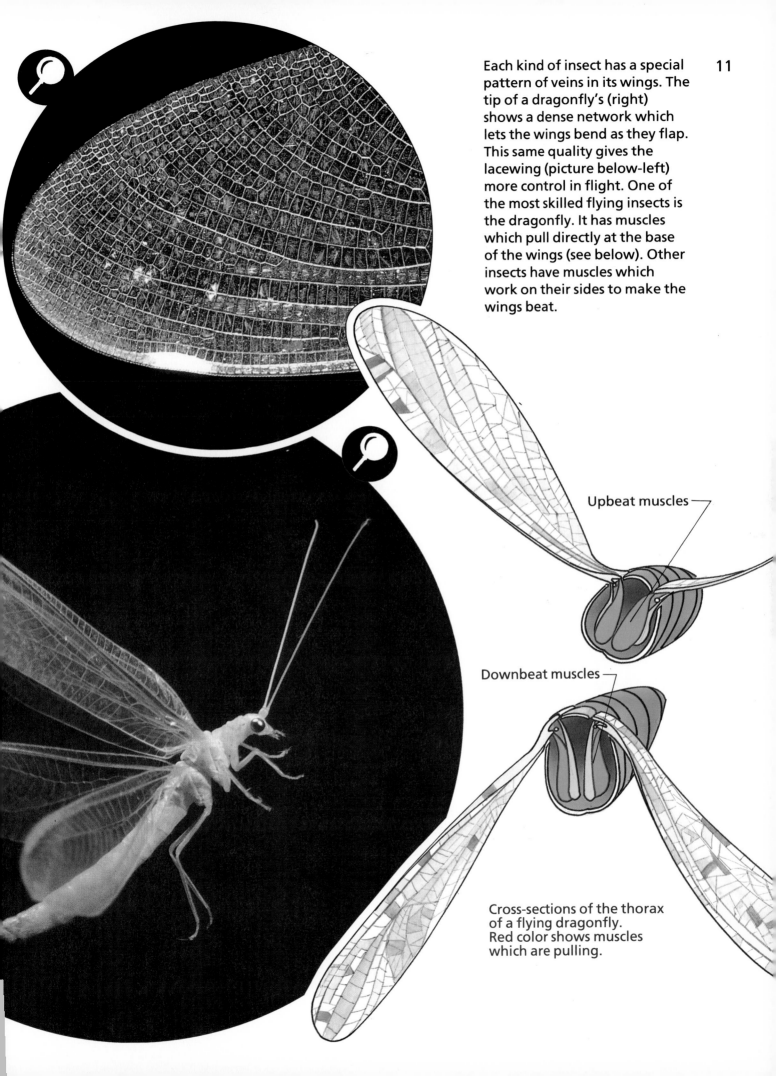

Each kind of insect has a special pattern of veins in its wings. The tip of a dragonfly's (right) shows a dense network which lets the wings bend as they flap. This same quality gives the lacewing (picture below-left) more control in flight. One of the most skilled flying insects is the dragonfly. It has muscles which pull directly at the base of the wings (see below). Other insects have muscles which work on their sides to make the wings beat.

Upbeat muscles

Downbeat muscles

Cross-sections of the thorax of a flying dragonfly. Red color shows muscles which are pulling.

THE BREATHING SYSTEM

Since an insect's body is an exoskeleton covered with waxy layers it cannot "breathe" through its skin as humans and other animals do. It does not carry oxygen in its bloodstream either. Instead, insects have a system of air-pipes, called tracheae, which allow them to breathe (see illustration below-left). These tracheae branch into smaller tracheoles, or air-tubes, which carry oxygen to the muscles and other organs. They are lined with a thin skin of chitin, the same material which makes up the exoskeleton, to protect them. Each also has spirals inside to strengthen it (see illustration lower-right). The tracheae form a complicated, branched breathing system throughout the insect's body and keep it alive.

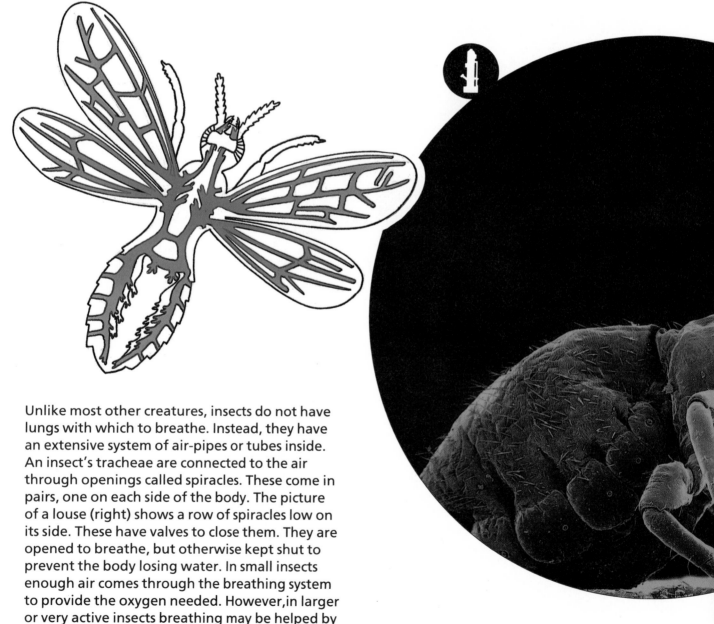

Unlike most other creatures, insects do not have lungs with which to breathe. Instead, they have an extensive system of air-pipes or tubes inside. An insect's tracheae are connected to the air through openings called spiracles. These come in pairs, one on each side of the body. The picture of a louse (right) shows a row of spiracles low on its side. These have valves to close them. They are opened to breathe, but otherwise kept shut to prevent the body losing water. In small insects enough air comes through the breathing system to provide the oxygen needed. However, in larger or very active insects breathing may be helped by pumping actions in the abdomen which suck in extra air.

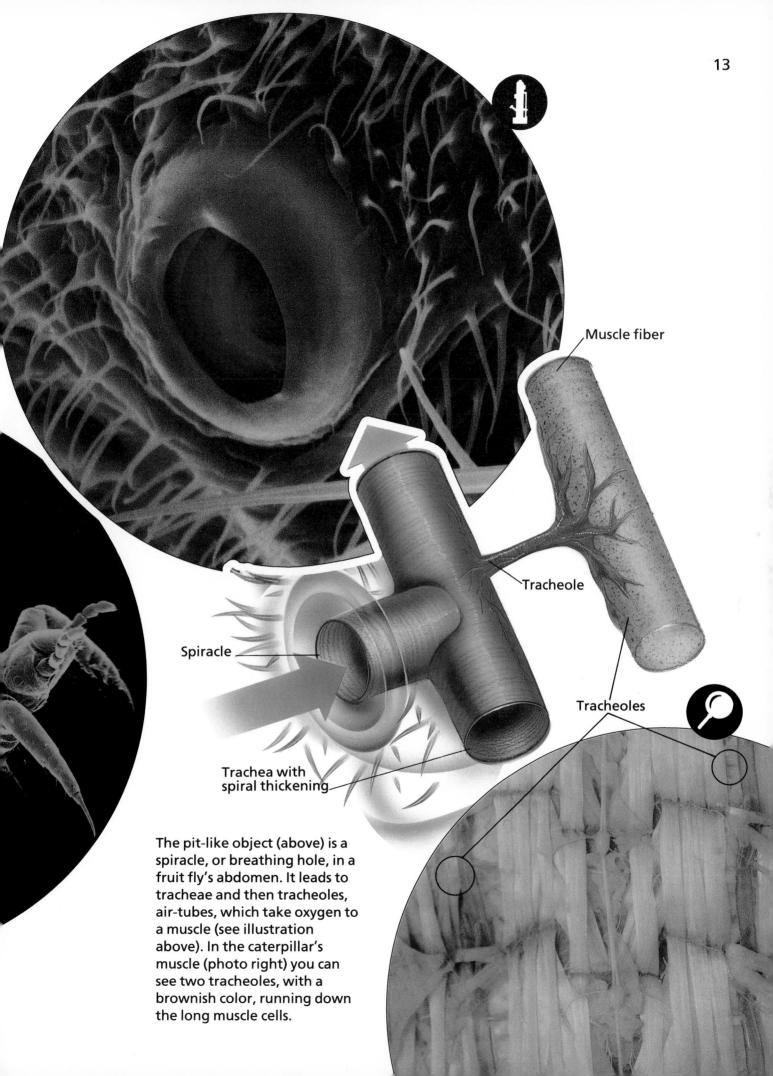

Muscle fiber

Tracheole

Spiracle

Tracheoles

Trachea with
spiral thickening

The pit-like object (above) is a
spiracle, or breathing hole, in a
fruit fly's abdomen. It leads to
tracheae and then tracheoles,
air-tubes, which take oxygen to
a muscle (see illustration
above). In the caterpillar's
muscle (photo right) you can
see two tracheoles, with a
brownish color, running down
the long muscle cells.

SUCKING MOUTHPARTS

Some insects only feed on liquids. They have mouths shaped like drinking straws which they use to suck their food through. Butterflies and moths are good examples of this. They both have a pair of mouthparts called maxillae. These zip together to form a long tube which can be pushed into a flower to suck up nectar. When not in use this tube is curled up under the head. If you watch butterflies you may see it in action. It is usually as long as the insect's favourite food flower. The worker honeybee also has mouthparts which form a tube for sucking nectar. The tip is wider and can move around, so it is called the "honey-spoon." However, the most common insects with sucking mouthpaths are flies.

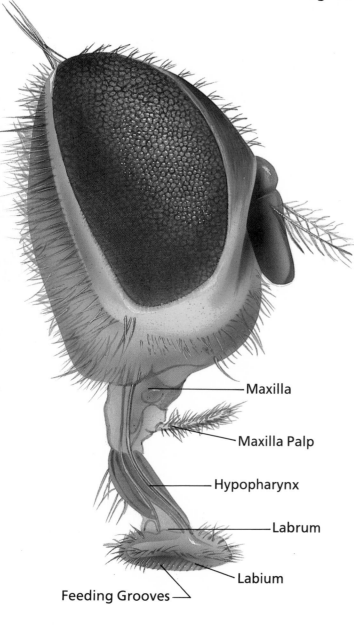

Maxilla

Maxilla Palp

Hypopharynx

Labrum

Labium

Feeding Grooves

Flies, such as the bluebottle above, are liquid feeders. This means they may have to use saliva to dissolve solid food into something they can suck up. Looking at the side of a fly's head (see illustration-left) you can see that its mouth is a complicated sucking tube. This proboscis, as it is called, is made up of the labrum, part of the mouth, and the labium, which can be pushed out into two flat lips. Running down to this is the hypopharynx, which carries saliva. The pictures on the right show these sucking mouthparts from below. We can see that the lips have grooves. These form a sort of sponge into which the food is sucked before going up the labrum.

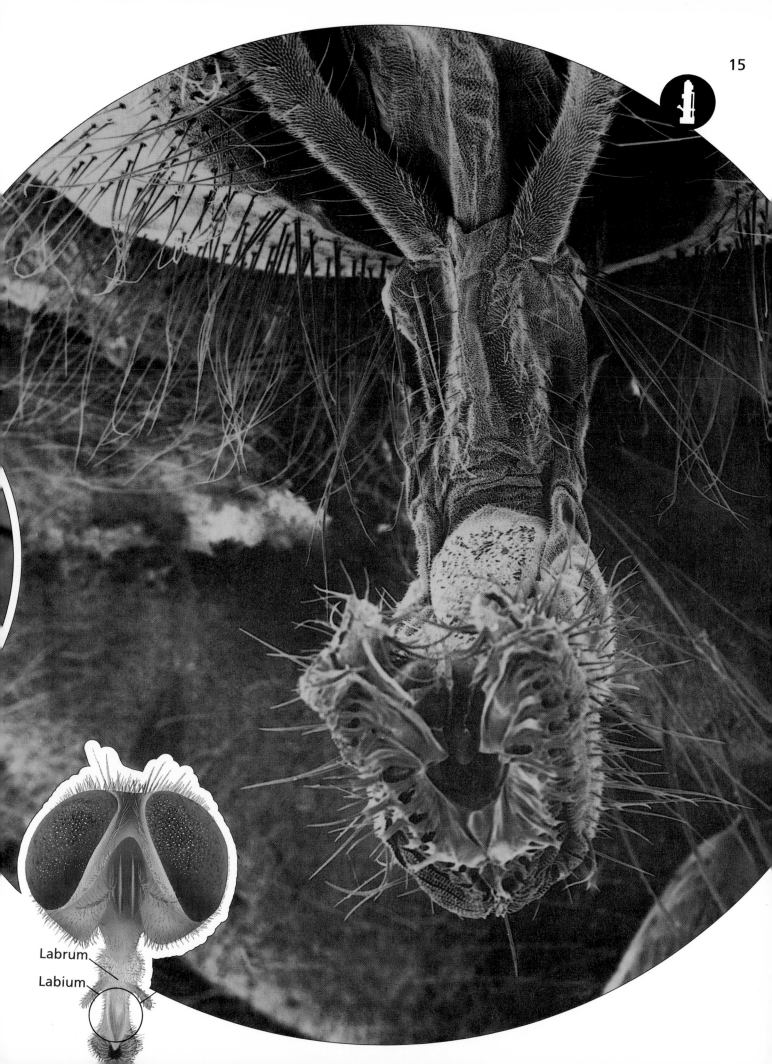

Labrum

Labium

PIERCING AND BITING MOUTHPARTS

Several kinds of insects have mouthparts that pierce. These include blood-hunters, like mosquitoes and gnats, and plant-suckers like aphids. They have needle-like jaws called mandibles and maxillae, covered by the labium (see illustration below-left). Inside of this tube two channels run down. One takes saliva down the maxilla while the insect can suck food up through the other one. But biting mouthparts are more common. Cockroaches, wasps, grasshoppers and dragonflies, for example, all bite their food. Some insects can even bite through wood or metal. Leg-like "palps" work around the mouth to feel and taste food, or to push it towards chewing jaws.

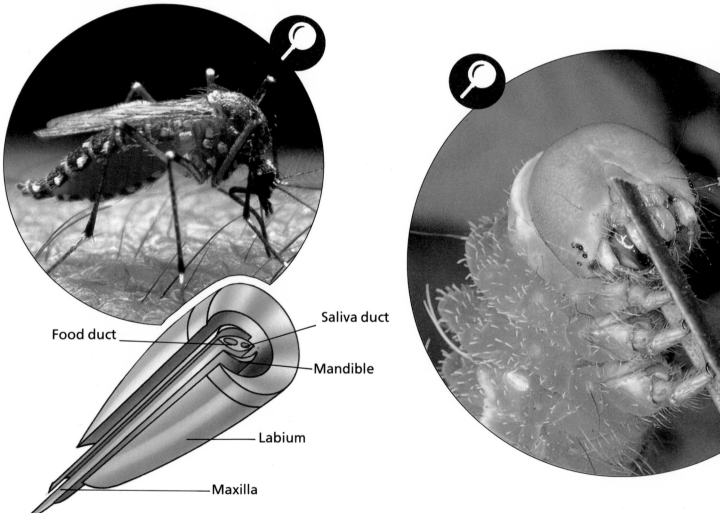

Food duct

Saliva duct

Mandible

Labium

Maxilla

A female mosquito, see picture above, can have piercing mouthparts up to 3mm (⅛th inch) long. This is strong enough to get through an animal's hide so that the insect can suck blood. Male mosquitoes have smaller mouthparts and cannot do this. They have to feed off the nectar in flowers.

Caterpillars, like the one in the picture above, may have soft bodies but their mouthparts are so good at biting and chewing that they are often thought of as a garden pest. Some eat their own eggshell after they hatch, but all kinds will consume large amounts of greenery as they grow.

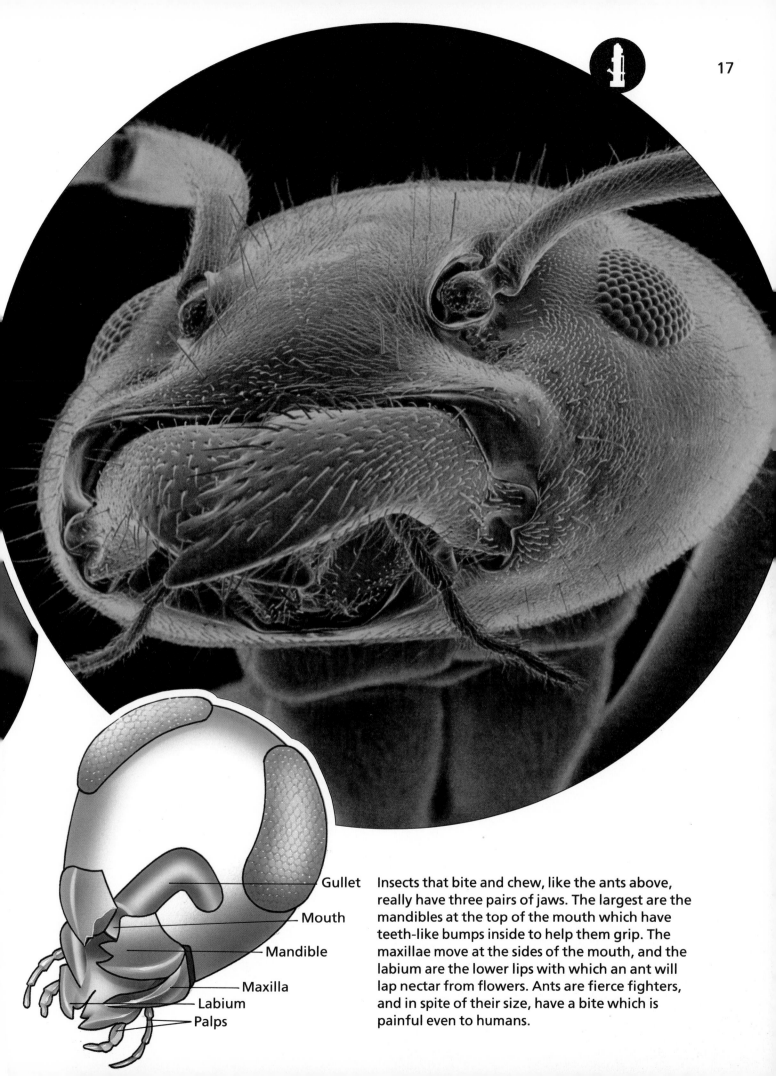

Gullet

Mouth

Mandible

Maxilla

Labium

Palps

Insects that bite and chew, like the ants above, really have three pairs of jaws. The largest are the mandibles at the top of the mouth which have teeth-like bumps inside to help them grip. The maxillae move at the sides of the mouth, and the labium are the lower lips with which an ant will lap nectar from flowers. Ants are fierce fighters, and in spite of their size, have a bite which is painful even to humans.

INSECT SENSES

Insects have the same five senses that we do, but their organs of touch, taste, smell, sight and hearing look very different from ours. For example, the ears of a cricket are like tiny drums on its front legs, and the antennae of a moth, illustrated on the left, resemble feathers. Some insects, such as butterflies, can taste with their feet. When they land on a surface they taste it to tell whether it is worth staying to feed. Often the sense organs are "tuned in" to only those things that are vital for survival. On the other hand, some insects can see things that we cannot. For example, bees can see ultraviolet light. This helps them gather nectar since certain flowers are easier for them to spot that way.

A fly has hundreds of eyes in its head (picture-left). They notice everything that moves nearby.

The antennae of an insect are one of its most important organs since they are used for smelling and feeling their surroundings. The male moth, pictured on the right, has impressive-looking, feathery antennae which can detect the scent of a female from over a kilometer (half a mile) away. These antennae also help the insect find food.

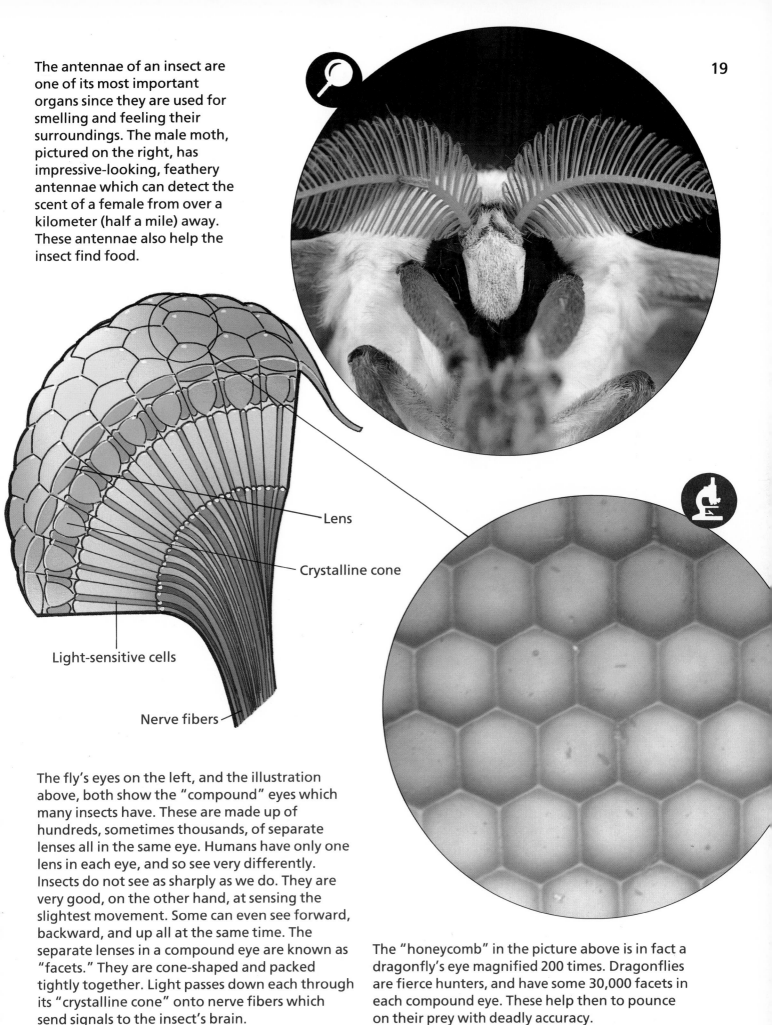

Lens

Crystalline cone

Light-sensitive cells

Nerve fibers

The fly's eyes on the left, and the illustration above, both show the "compound" eyes which many insects have. These are made up of hundreds, sometimes thousands, of separate lenses all in the same eye. Humans have only one lens in each eye, and so see very differently. Insects do not see as sharply as we do. They are very good, on the other hand, at sensing the slightest movement. Some can even see forward, backward, and up all at the same time. The separate lenses in a compound eye are known as "facets." They are cone-shaped and packed tightly together. Light passes down each through its "crystalline cone" onto nerve fibers which send signals to the insect's brain.

The "honeycomb" in the picture above is in fact a dragonfly's eye magnified 200 times. Dragonflies are fierce hunters, and have some 30,000 facets in each compound eye. These help then to pounce on their prey with deadly accuracy.

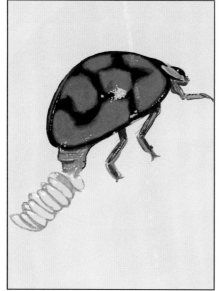

REPRODUCTION AND GROWTH

The adult life of many insects is short, only a few days or weeks long. The main task of the adults is to find a mate and to produce young. After mating, the female lays her eggs (see the ladybird illustrated on left), which have a tough shell and are waterproof to help them survive harsh conditions. The insect that hatches usually looks very different from its parents. It will not have wings and has to go through a process of change (called metamorphosis) before it becomes an adult. It also has to grow, which is difficult because its exoskeleton cannot expand as it gets bigger. So an insect must shed its old skin when it grows, stretching quickly before the new one, waiting underneath, has time to harden.

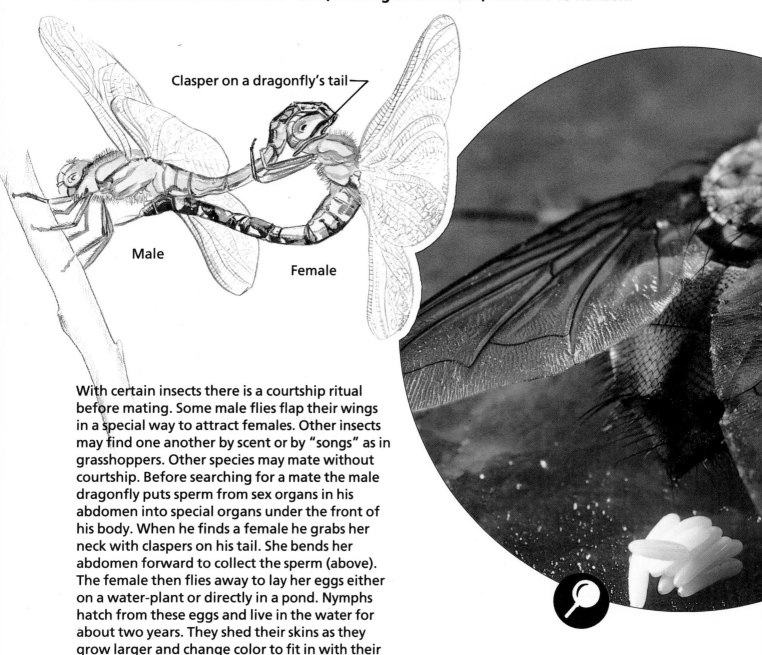

Clasper on a dragonfly's tail

Male

Female

With certain insects there is a courtship ritual before mating. Some male flies flap their wings in a special way to attract females. Other insects may find one another by scent or by "songs" as in grasshoppers. Other species may mate without courtship. Before searching for a mate the male dragonfly puts sperm from sex organs in his abdomen into special organs under the front of his body. When he finds a female he grabs her neck with claspers on his tail. She bends her abdomen forward to collect the sperm (above). The female then flies away to lay her eggs either on a water-plant or directly in a pond. Nymphs hatch from these eggs and live in the water for about two years. They shed their skins as they grow larger and change color to fit in with their surroundings until they emerge as adults.

The picture (above-left) shows a female bluebottle fly laying her eggs on some meat. The young that hatch (called maggots) must have have plenty of food close by. They are not able to travel very far, unlike their parents, and will feed on this flesh for the first stage of their lives.

On the surface of a nasturtium leaf (above) you can see the sculptured eggshells of a large white butterfly. The eggs are laid in batches of up to 100, and hatch after 5 to 20 days. You can see where the caterpillar has chewed its way out of one egg. It will feed and grow for about 30 days.

INCOMPLETE METAMORPHOSIS

Most insects hatch from eggs and will go through stages of growth. Some do not change their shape as much as others, only their size. Cockroaches and grasshoppers, for example, go through what is known as an incomplete metamorphosis. As they grow they have to shed their old skin. This is called molting. As you can see in illustrations below, an aphid changes size and shape gradually with each molt. Even before it is a full adult the wing-buds can be seen. Finally, the wings grow to full size, and the insect is ready to reproduce. Insects that grow in this way usually live in the same sort of place, and feed on the same type of food, throughout their lives. Young insects of this kind are known as nymphs.

The photograph on the right shows an adult female aphid with some aphid nymphs. All of these bugs suck juices from the plants they live on. Many kinds of aphid lay eggs in spring which grow into wingless adults by the summer. These can give birth to live young instead of laying eggs. Millions of nymphs are produced in this way, and aphids become a pest in our gardens. If you look closely at a leaf infested with aphids (a rosebush would be a good example) you will observe the insects in many different sizes. You might also see empty cast skins (photo above-right) which have been molted by nymphs. They may still be attached to the leaf by their mouthparts. You might even see large females giving birth. Only when fall comes are winged adults that lay eggs produced again, and the numbers of aphids around will start to decline.

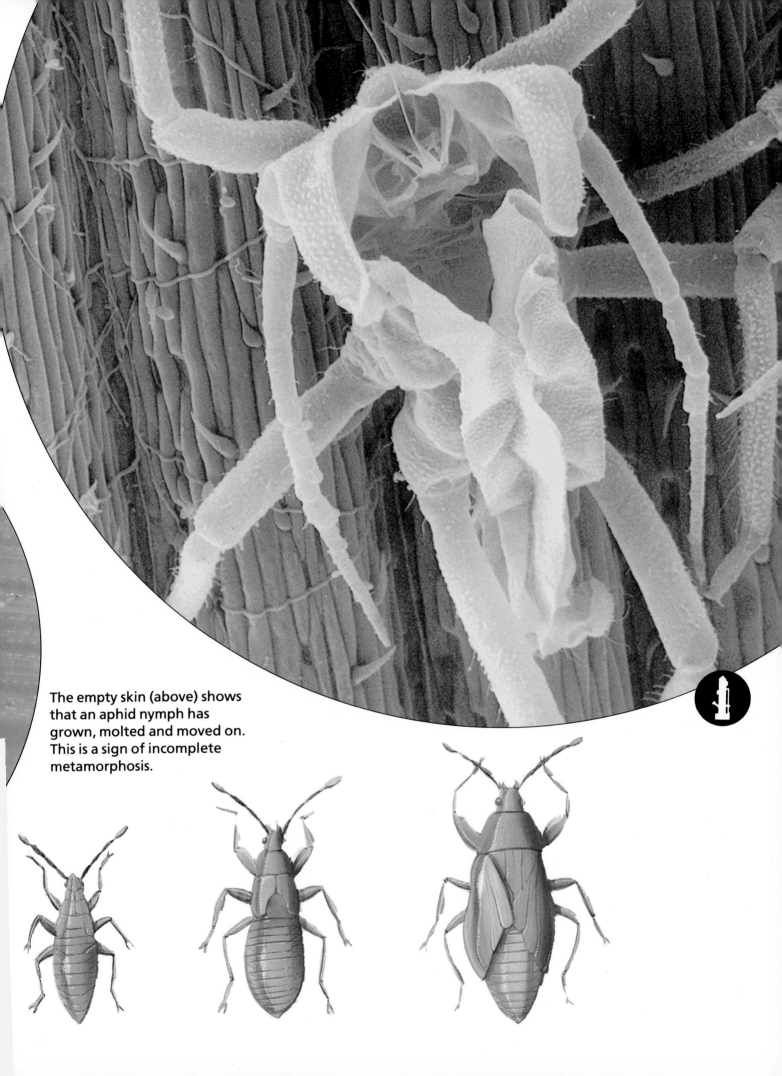

The empty skin (above) shows that an aphid nymph has grown, molted and moved on. This is a sign of incomplete metamorphosis.

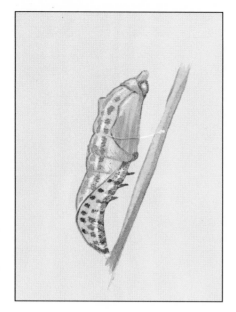

COMPLETE METAMORPHOSIS

Insects that undergo complete metamorphosis have offspring which look completely different from their parents. The young live apart and even feed on other types of food. Also, their wings do not normally appear until they can emerge as adults. However, most important of all, these creatures have to progress to a stage where they appear to be resting in a silky cocoon or chrysalis. During this period, called pupation, they do not move anywhere but a tremendous change takes place inside. The insect's body is completely broken down and rebuilt into a new form. Many insects, such as ants, moths, flies, butterflies, bees, and beetles undergo complete metamorphosis.

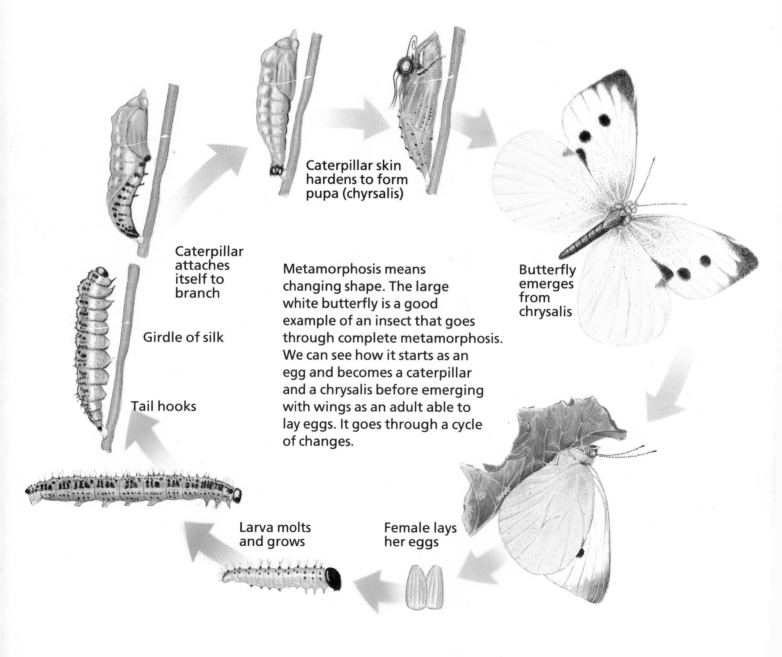

Caterpillar skin hardens to form pupa (chyrsalis)

Caterpillar attaches itself to branch

Girdle of silk

Tail hooks

Metamorphosis means changing shape. The large white butterfly is a good example of an insect that goes through complete metamorphosis. We can see how it starts as an egg and becomes a caterpillar and a chrysalis before emerging with wings as an adult able to lay eggs. It goes through a cycle of changes.

Butterfly emerges from chrysalis

Larva molts and grows

Female lays her eggs

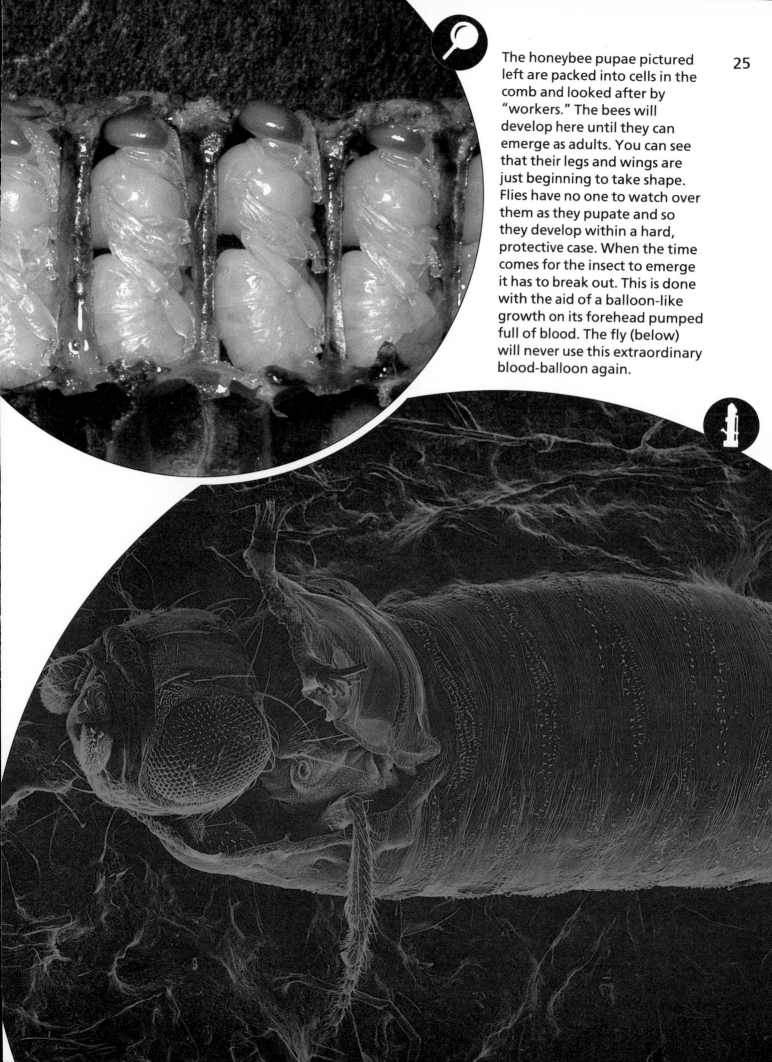

The honeybee pupae pictured left are packed into cells in the comb and looked after by "workers." The bees will develop here until they can emerge as adults. You can see that their legs and wings are just beginning to take shape. Flies have no one to watch over them as they pupate and so they develop within a hard, protective case. When the time comes for the insect to emerge it has to break out. This is done with the aid of a balloon-like growth on its forehead pumped full of blood. The fly (below) will never use this extraordinary blood-balloon again.

INSECTS AS PESTS

There are millions of different kinds of insect in the world. Most do not bother us at all but some can cause harm and are known as pests. Some insects bite, like horseflies and mosquitoes. Others, like the flea shown on the left, live by sucking blood and can sometimes spread disease. Many insect pests, such as caterpillars or aphids, do not harm people directly but cause damage when they feed in our gardens by chewing away at leaves or sucking the life out of growing plants. Other insect pests eat crops once they have been gathered and put in storage. Beetles cause trouble in this way, particularly those known as weevils. Some pests can even attack our homes since they eat wood and will weaken roofs, floors and stairs.

Woodworm are the larvae, or young , of a beetle. They tunnel into and feed on wood before they pupate. In the photo on the right we can see an adult beetle emerging from its telltale hole after complete metamorphosis.

There are two types of human louse. One lives on the head (see photo below) and can be an itchy nuisance if it lays its sticky eggs (called nits) in your hair. The other kind of louse lives on the body and can spread serious diseases when it bites you.

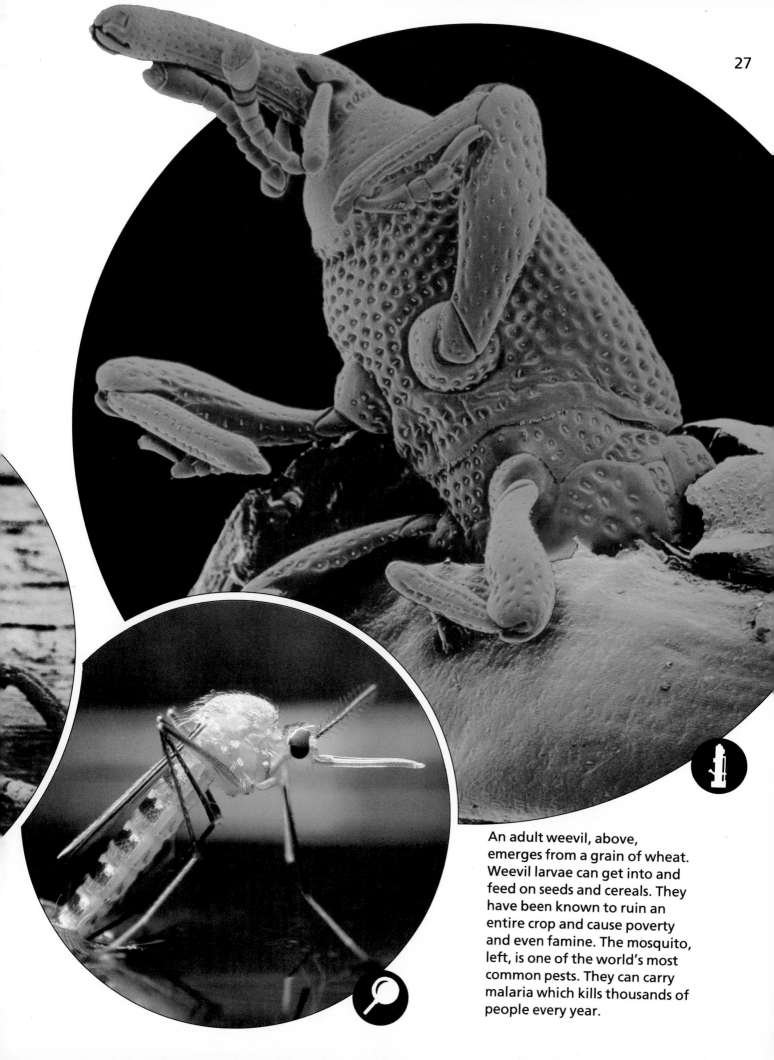

An adult weevil, above, emerges from a grain of wheat. Weevil larvae can get into and feed on seeds and cereals. They have been known to ruin an entire crop and cause poverty and even famine. The mosquito, left, is one of the world's most common pests. They can carry malaria which kills thousands of people every year.

PRACTICAL PROJECTS

You can discover a lot about nature's miniature world with just a magnifying glass. But to see more you will need a standard microscope. Anything you want to study must be mounted on a glass slide. These should be delicate insects, or parts of insect , which you can see through. But you can also make slides of cells from inside the insect's body. To do this you need special dyes to stain your specimen so that your eye can pick out different cells. The way to do this is outlined below. If you are going to try something difficult, it is worth asking for help from an experienced adult, perhaps at school. Some microscope suppliers will supply slides ready-made. These are often of excellent quality and not expensive.

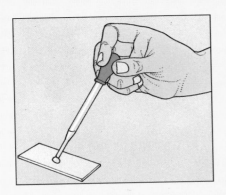

To prepare a slide of cells, place a drop of clean water containing them on the glass.

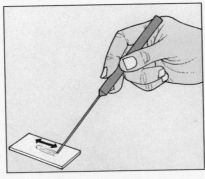

With a wire loop that has been sterilized in a flame, spread the fluid thinly and let it dry.

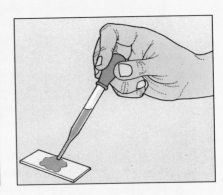

Add a small drop of staining dye to the cells and leave for a few minutes.

Wash off the dye with water or alcohol. You can stain with another, contrasting dye.

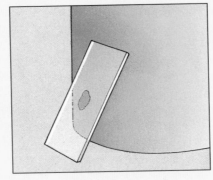

Leave the slide to dry. You can speed up drying by warming the slide over a flame.

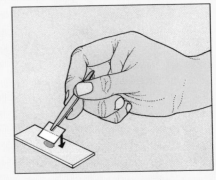

Place the cover slip (a thin square of glass) over the stained cells.

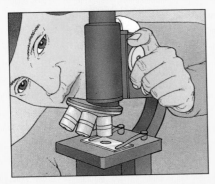

Put the slide on the microscope stage and position the mirror to give you good illumination.

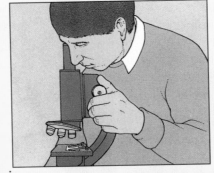

Select the objective lens you want, then move the eyepiece up or down to focus.

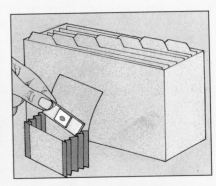

Keep your prepared slides in a cardboard wallet made from a thin sheet of cardboard.

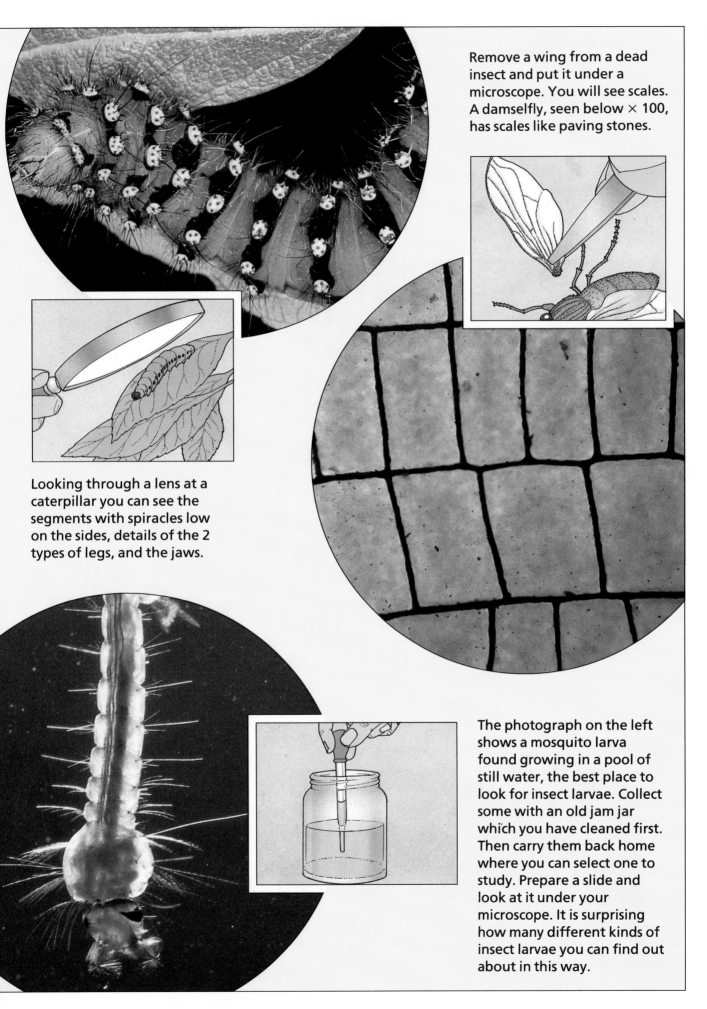

Remove a wing from a dead insect and put it under a microscope. You will see scales. A damselfly, seen below × 100, has scales like paving stones.

Looking through a lens at a caterpillar you can see the segments with spiracles low on the sides, details of the 2 types of legs, and the jaws.

The photograph on the left shows a mosquito larva found growing in a pool of still water, the best place to look for insect larvae. Collect some with an old jam jar which you have cleaned first. Then carry them back home where you can select one to study. Prepare a slide and look at it under your microscope. It is surprising how many different kinds of insect larvae you can find out about in this way.

MICROPHOTOGRAPHY

Some of the photographs in this book were taken using a camera with close-up lenses (called macrolenses) that magnify the subject in much the same way as a magnifying glass would, only they sometimes allow us to take an even closer view. Others with greater magnification, like the dragonfly's eye on page 19, were taken by fitting a camera to the eyepiece of a scientific microscope. Such photos are known as photomicrographs. The colors in these are often stains rather than natural. If you have a microscope you can take your own photomicrographs. You will need a single lens reflex camera and a special camera attachment. Many images in this book were produced using scanning electron microscopes.

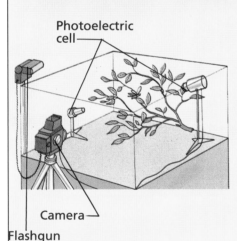

You can take close-up photos of insects using an all-glass aquarium. But special equipment is needed for sharp pictures of insects in flight, including powerful flashguns triggered by photoelectric cells.

There are two main types of electron microscope. In a transmission type, a beam of electrons is passed through an extremely thin slice of tissue and an image is produced on a viewing screen. On a scanning electron microscope (an SEM), a fine beam of electrons is moved across the surface of the tissue for reflections to be collected and used to create an image on a television type of screen. Using an SEM, realistic 3-D images are produced. But as with all types of microscope specimens, the tissues and organs are no longer alive. The slide preparation process kills live cells. The photos produced by an SEM have false colors added in processing.

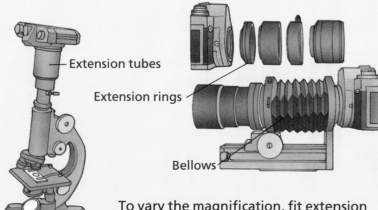

To vary the magnification, fit extension rings or bellows to the camera attachment.

GLOSSARY

antennae the feelers on an insect's head. They contain tiny sense organs concerned with touch, smell, "taste," for detecting temperature or moisture.

cells the tiny units or building blocks with which living things are made.

chitin a substance related to sugar that makes up to 50 percent of an insect's skin.

chrysalis the pupa of a butterfly, the stage that occurs between caterpillar and adult.

clasper an organ used by an animal to hold its mate while mating takes place, as the claspers on the end of the male dragonfly's abdomen.

duct a tube down which liquids flow in an animal's body.

egg the female reproductive cell.

larva young insect which has hatched from its egg and must become a pupa.

maggot a larva such as that of many flies, which has no legs and moves by wriggling. The head is poorly developed and usually at the narrow end of the maggot.

magnification the number of times larger across that an object seen through a lens or microscope appears compared with its true size.

metamorphosis an obvious change of body shape and structure that takes place during the life of an animal.

molting the way that young insects that go through incomplete metamorphosis shed their skins in order to grow bigger.

nymph young insects which have hatched from eggs and must undergo incomplete metamorphosis.

photoelectric a device that produces a small current of electricity when light is shone on it, switching off when the light is interrupted. Photoelectric cells can be used to trigger cameras when a light beam is interrupted by an animal going through it.

pigment a substance that is colored. Pigments provide some of the colors of insect skins, but other insect colors are produced by the way light is reflected from their surfaces.

pro-leg a fleshy cone-shaped bump that sticks out under the abdomen of a caterpillar and helps it move. Prolegs can often be pulled back into the abdomen. They are not forerunners of any legs in the adult, unlike the three pairs of legs on the thorax.

proboscis any long extension of the head which looks like a "nose," although its functions may not be nose-like. The proboscis of a moth is made up of its mouthparts and forms a drinking straw.

pupa the apparently quiet stage in the complete metamorphosis of an insect.

reproduction to produce young or offspring.

setae tiny hairs on an insect's body which can act as sense organs.

sperm the male's reproductive cells which must fertilize the female's egg before offspring can be produced.

system a set of organs and tissues that work together to do a particular job for the body.

WEIGHTS AND MEASURES

mm = millimeter 10mm = 1cm = 4/10 inch
cm = centimeter 100cm = 1m = 3 feet
m = meter 1000m = 1km = 6/10 mile
km = kilometer
lb = pound

g = gram 1000g = 1kg = 2lb 3oz
kg = kilogram
0.1 = 1/10
0.01 = 1/100
0.001 = 1/1000

INDEX

abdomen 6, 8, 12, 18, 20
antennae 6, 7, 19, 27, 31
ants 7, 16, 17, 24, 26
aphids 16, 22, 26

bees 8, 18, 24
beetle, water 29
beetles 8, 10, 24, 26
biting 16, 17
blood 12, 25
bluebottle 14, 21
body 6, 24
breathing 12
bugs 16, 22
butterflies 10, 14, 18, 21, 24

capsule 7, 31
caterpillar 8, 13, 16, 26, 27, 29
chitin 6, 31
chrysalis 24, 31
clasper 20, 31
claws 8, 9
cockroaches 10, 16, 22
color 10
courtship 20
cricket 18

diseases 16, 26
dragonflies 10, 11, 16, 19, 20

ears 18
egg-laying tube 6
eggs 20, 21, 22, 24, 25
eggshell 16, 20, 21
exoskeleton 6, 7, 10, 20
eyes 6, 19

feet 8, 9
femur 8
flea 9, 26
flies 8, 10, 14, 18, 19, 20, 24, 25

fly, fruit 13, 25
flying 10, 11
food and feeding 14, 16, 17, 18,
   21, 22, 26, 29

gnats 16
grasshopper 8, 16, 18, 20, 22
growing 20
gullet 17
gut 6

head 6, 7, 14, 19
honeybee 14, 25
hooks 8, 10
horsefly 26
housefly 9

image 4

jaws 16, 17, 27, 29

labium 14, 16, 17
labrum 14
lacewings 10, 11
larvae 24, 25, 26, 27, 29
legs 6, 8, 29
lenses 4
locust 8
louse, human 12, 26

maggot 21, 24, 31
magnification 4, 5, 31
magnifying glass 4
mandibles 16, 17, 29
maxillae 14, 16, 17
metamorphosis 20, 22, 24, 31
microscopes, types of 4, 5, 8, 30
mosquitoes 16, 26
moths 10, 14, 19, 29
moulting 22, 24
mouthparts 6, 7, 14, 16, 22

muscles 11, 12, 13

nits 26
nymphs 22

oxygen 12

pads 8, 9
palps 17
pigment 31
proboscis 14, 31
pro-legs 8, 31
pulvilli 8, 9
pupa 24, 25

reproduction 20, 22
reproductive organs 6

saliva 16
salivary duct 14, 16
scales 10, 29
senses 6, 8, 10, 18, 19
setae 6, 8
skin 6, 12, 20, 22, 25
spiracles 12, 29
sting 6, 26

termite 6, 26
thorax 6, 8, 10, 11
tibia 8
tracheae 12, 13

valves 12
veins 10, 11, 31

wasps 16, 17, 26
weevils 26, 27
wings 6, 10, 11, 20, 22, 24, 29
woodworm 26

Photographic Credits:
Cover and pages 7, 8, 9t, 10, 11t, 13, 14, 16,
17, 18, 19l, 20, 21, 23, 25b, 26, 27, 29m and
b and 31r: Science Photo Library; pages
6-7, 9b, 11b, 12-13, 15, 19r, 22, 25t, 29t and
31t: Biophoto Associates.

PRINTED IN BELGIUM BY

proost
INTERNATIONAL BOOK PRODUCTION